Underwater Spiders

Written by Jo Windsor

Some spiders can live under the water.
This is an underwater spider.
It lives in a pond.
It is very good at swimming.

This spider makes a web
under the water.
It makes a web
in the plants.
The web is its home.

But... the spider has to have air.
It swims to the top of
the water to get the air.
It holds the air on its body.
The air is trapped
on the spider's body
in a bubble.

The spider takes the air bubble down to its web.
It swims up and down to its web lots of times.
Now it has a lot of air in its web.

The spider's web is like a net.
The air bubble cannot get out.
The spider can stay
in its bubble for
a long time.
Sometimes it will stay
in its bubble
all winter!

The spider looks for its food
under the water.
It likes to eat small fish.
It likes to eat insects, too.
The spider gets the food
with its legs.
It takes the food
into its web
to eat.

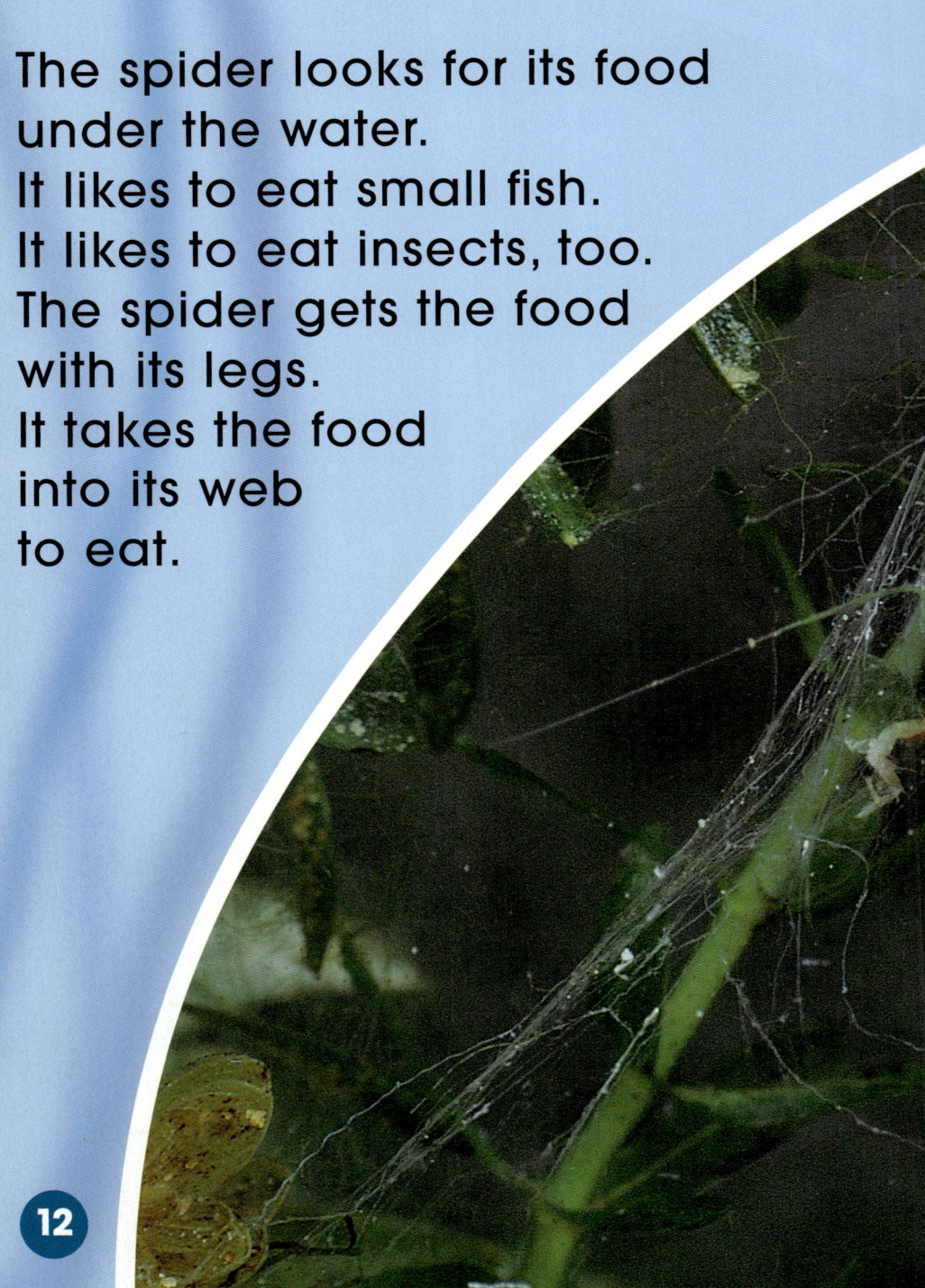

The spider lays her eggs under the water.
She lays lots of eggs.
She keeps her eggs in her bubble under the water.

Index

air bubble .. 6, 8, 10, 14

eggs 14

getting air 6, 8

getting food 12

swimming 2, 6, 8

web 4, 8, 10, 12

Guide Notes

Title: Underwater Spiders
Stage: Early (4) – Green

Genre: Non-Fiction (Expository)
Approach: Guided Reading
Processes: Thinking Critically, Exploring Language, Processing Information
Written and Visual Focus: Photographs (static images), Labels, Index

THINKING CRITICALLY
(sample questions)
- Look at the title and read it to the children. Ask: "What do you think this book is going to tell us?"
- Ask the children what they know about underwater spiders.
- Focus the children's attention on the Index. Ask: "What are you going to find out about in this book?"
- If you want to find out about air bubbles, what pages would you look on?
- If you want to find out about getting food, what page would you look on?
- Look at pages 6 and 7. Why do you think the spider has to swim up and down for air lots of times?
- Look at pages 12 and 13. Why do you think the spider takes the food back to its web to eat?

EXPLORING LANGUAGE

Terminology
Title, cover, photographs, author, photographers

Vocabulary
Interest words: underwater, pond, web, trapped, bubble
High-frequency word (new): lots
Compound words: underwater, cannot, sometimes
Positional words: under, up, top, down

Print Conventions
Capital letter for sentence beginnings, full stops, commas, exclamation mark, ellipsis